VAGINA VIBES

A MANDALA COLORING JOURNEY

A Sex Therapy Tool for Embracing and Celebrating Feminine Beauty

Idea and Overseen : M. Kazem Najafi
Illustrations: Kosar Dodange
Captions: Maryam Sadat Hesami
Translation (Persian to English): Negin Gorganinezhad

Foreword

Welcome to «Vagina Vibes: A Mandala Coloring Journey» a unique blend of art and therapy designed to foster understanding, appreciation, and healing. Within these pages, 25 intricate illustrations celebrate the beauty and complexity of the female genitalia. Each mandala is a canvas for coloring and a pathway to embracing and celebrating feminine essence and sexual health.

This book is more than just a collection of drawings; it is a tool for sex therapy and art therapy aimed at helping individuals—men and women alike—nurture positive attitudes towards female genitalia. By engaging creatively with these illustrations, we hope you will embark on a journey of self-discovery, empowerment, and acceptance.

Acknowledgments

We extend our heartfelt gratitude to the talented individuals whose dedication made this book possible:

Kosar Dodange: Your artistic vision and skill brought each mandala to life, capturing the essence of beauty and intricacy.

Maryam Sadat Hesami: Your thoughtful and evocative captions enriched the experience, providing deeper insights into each illustration.

Negin Gorganinezhad: Thank you for translating the original text from Persian to English, ensuring accessibility to a broader audience.

Zahra Alizadeh|Faeze Aliakbari|Nikoo Jafari: We are indebted to the contributions of our sexology experts who guided the conceptualization and selection of themes, ensuring that each illustration embodies principles of sexual health and positivity.

Your collaborative efforts have created a transformative tool that will, we believe, inspire healing, empowerment, and a renewed appreciation for the diversity and uniqueness of female anatomy.

* * *

We would love to hear about your journey with ‹Vagina Vibes: A Mandala Coloring Journey.' Please share your thoughts and experiences with us via email:
Contact @kamazischool.com

My mysterious garden...

Here is wonderland.

Like a winding maze, full of mystery!

Or like a mansion, beautiful and full of many surprises!

At the entrance of this mysterious garden, there is an organ called clitoris, which makes entering this land easier and easier. At this moment, outside the mansion, two people are talking to each other.

Listen! They are expressing their love to each other. The sound of their whispering in ear and holding hands and kissing comes this far. Now this corridor becomes slightly damp in honor of these pure moments and is ready to deepen their love...

After the entrance, you now enter a hallway that may be a bit narrow. Like a foyer to enter the main hall where important events happen.

When you look from a distance, there are two corridors on the left and right sides of this garden, each of which has the task of releasing an egg from the ovary, and the small and young egg, like the seed of a flower or fruit, comes to the uterus and is placed in a warm and soft bed. Wait for the sperm that is supposed to arrive from the same lovers. Maybe an embryo will be created from them and the same beautiful miracle will happen. Maybe, according to every month's schedule, with a natural washing called period or menstrual habit, you can wash and remove these events from this garden. Dredge the clay and paving stones of this building. And again, day after day...

I love my mysterious organ, my uterus. I think about every single thing she does quietly. All these events are for me to be a human being and a woman. Like me, put your hand on your stomach right now and be grateful for it.

With chocolate sauce and Smarties? No thanks.

Thanks...no need!

Wait! Once you savor it, you'll feel its unique taste—like no other. You can't give her an example.

You can't say it tastes like chocolate or that kind of fruit.

No way! You can't find something like this. It seems idle!

Just think about the first time you savored the Persimmon. Or banana, or even coffee, you remember?

Or think about a closer memory, like tasting avocado

What did it taste like?

Could you say that this fruit has a familiar taste?

Sometimes, it seems anything is supposed to have its taste. This world is so big that we expect new tastes, smells, and colors daily. Sometimes, discovering our partner's body is full of novelty, like conquering a new world. How sweet it is to find the corners of this land, spending time and patience to feel and perceive this new world, part of which is its unique tastes and smells. A friend used to say: I can never taste peanuts. But once or twice, at the insistence of his friends, he tried peanut shake in a cafe. I saw him today. His face was full of boils. He said: I eat only peanut butter for breakfast every day! His was changed!

We are used to familiar tastes and smells!

We easily miss the chance to experience new flavors,

Unfortunately, our eyes and minds have learned to assume that food is delicious when coated with colored and harmful chocolates.

Let's not get away from the new and unknown topic.

The vagina can also have its unique taste, like persimmons or anything else. You can imagine it, whatever it is, like a newly discovered fruit on an unknown island. See it well, smell it, and taste it little by little. With chocolate sauce and Smarties?

No thanks. No need, thanks.

Symmetrical or asymmetrical?

My eyes are blurry.

In the distance, I see a woman in a long dress with a particular model.

Her skirt caresses the ground, and the edges of her beautiful dress dance back and forth with each step. It is as if a net or something similar to chiffon is tied to the crown of her head, which is intertwined and woven from the back with the pleated edges of the dress to create a dreamy scene at the bottom of the dress.

Despite the inconsistency and asymmetry, it has created a fantastic harmony!

That's when my opinion about using «incongruent» and «asymmetrical» for this image changed forever. I now only saw symmetry and beauty.

As I get closer, I see a vagina that looks like a beautiful goddess whose presence is soothing.

With that special appearance and creation, it is as if she was created to embrace Phallus warmly with every part of her being and receive deep love with all of this beautiful dress she wears.

She can even be seen as a butterfly that spreads its wings to embrace its friend or protects its internal organs with folded wings when alone and without a hug.

Anyway, now I see a vagina walking in a beautiful dress!

No matter what angle I look at, I do not see this creation without wisdom.

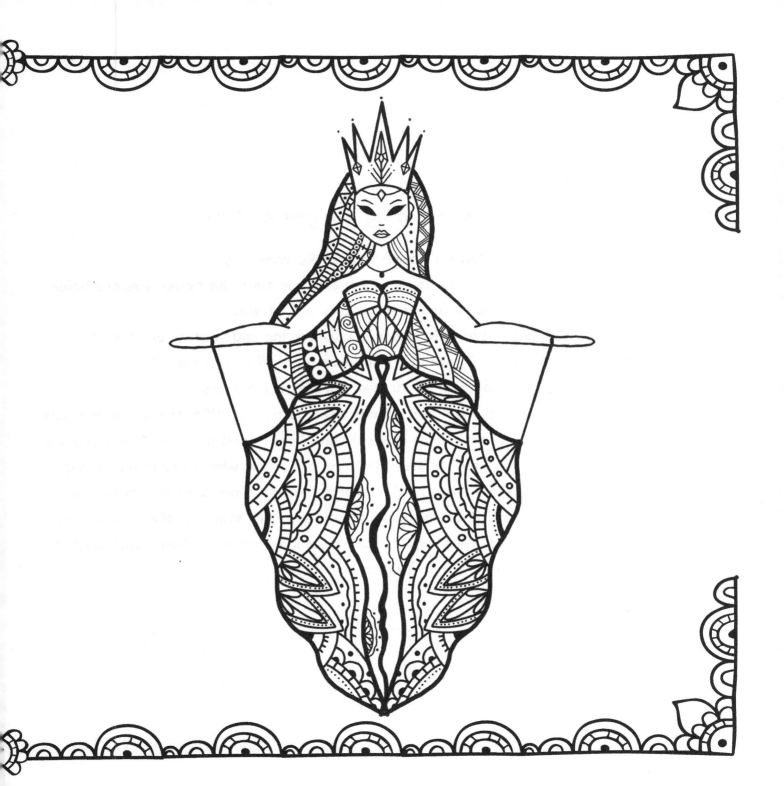

This flower is only for you and me!

I also have a flower that I like very much.

I have never seen someone like my flower. It is exciting that the flower you are holding is unique and there is only one of this.

It is exciting to know that this flower is only for me and that no one but my sweetheart, whom I love and who loves me, will see and smell it.

I want both of us to take care of our flowers.

Like when you know not all flowers in a garden need to be beautiful and unique for you! As if among all the flowers, your eyes saw only one flower, and only that one remained in your memory. I pressed my forehead to hers and softly whispered these to her.

It has a sense of mystery, like a unique floral fragrance wrapped in a cozy and beautiful corner. You know it belongs only to you and her, someone who is safe and dear to you and will be. Not that anyone, as a passerby, can visit there and smell its fragrance.

Unrivaled and always winning

Yes, I am standing here. On the winners' platform!

But there is no rival in this competition. Because whatever I am, I will be lovable and desirable in my way.

There is no competition or comparison here. Because all of us will be beautiful and unique in our way. Everyone here is supposed to shine on the podium. Because the first and second will be meaningless in our world, remember from us a world where we are all standing on the winners' steps based on our diversity and numbers.

The vagina is the organ that takes the body and soul to the party of pleasure and liberation; Why not win? It is evident that the vagina, the organ that is the place of exciting and miraculous events such as fertility and childbirth, has the highest and most exalted position.

The vagina is an intelligent and always-winning organ. It always stands on the first platform; you must know and discover it. You will be immersed in its secrets; you will be amazed by its wonders; you will be surprised at its creation.

The more you get to know her, the more you will love her. Yes, she is standing here. Right on the winning platform!

No news anywhere!

1 ..2 ..3..!

You hear me?

Let's face it: our minds need a significant overhaul.

Most of our shame, embarrassment, lack of self-confidence, failures, and disappointments are due to false and baseless beliefs.

We will reach nothing but hollow cans and brains if we root each one. They are nothing more than delusional mindsets!

Let's accept that sometimes this is comforting: There is no news anywhere!

For example, most beauty standards are determined by pharmaceutical and cosmetic companies to sell their products. Isn't it strange that these standards change from earth to heaven every few years?

In the meantime, you and I are running from one side to the other, looking for a mirage, so we never reach this caravan.

Let's accept that whatever we believe about ourselves will be the same belief and behavior that others will have toward us. So, instead of wasting time and only dealing with the surface layers, let's also think about our inner layers.

1... 2 ... 3..., you still hear my voice?

I wish you could hear my voice.

Thanks for all I have.

Thanks! Thanks, from the bottom of my heart.

Thanks for the pleasure I get.

Thanks for all I have.

Thanks for every sweet moment I give to myself and my sweetheart.

Thanks for the release of pleasure and uplifting hormones in my body and the sense of liberation of my soul.

Thanks for my body's pleasure, invigorating hormones, and my soul's liberation.

Here and now, I promise myself, as long as I live, to be grateful to have a dear organ like you. Everything in you is beautiful and appropriate, and thanks for that.

Look! The vagina can be like hands that are always grateful for experiencing and tasting the greatest pleasures in the world.

I think I will never forget this image.

I want to thank my creator and body for every sweet moment I spent remembering this picture.

Or

To take care of my body and vagina, like this picture that has her hands in the shape of a photo frame to hold a precious object.

I want to be careful and appreciative of the little treasure that is the foundation of my entry into the world of countless pleasures.

Even Thanks for remembering it.

Thanks, thanks to the moon and back!

You are a peacock too!

She thought «being ashamed» was always the positive side of the story and should be hidden from everyone.

On the other hand, she believed that the whole world was beautiful and appropriate, but I am only an awkward patch of existence if I am seen.

Everyone and everything she saw; she admired her with the beauty of words.

But when she came to herself, she would talk and bite her lips because she «didn't see herself.»

Just like a peacock that has not seen herself and is unaware of her indescribable beauty.

A peacock that is unaware of this irreplaceable creation of God.

How can a peacock that never opens its wings and does not show herself be distinguished from other fowls in the garden?

As if it is no different from any of the ordinary and straightforward birds that we pass by quickly!

Who knows how beautiful these beautiful and desirable feathers are hidden in layers of gray feathers? Look at this peacock. Now you spread your wings and know that showing off is so enjoyable that if the look of «the one who should» reaches you, you will say:

I wish I had spread my wings and expressed myself earlier.

That's what you see in the mirror.

It's me.

A vagina.

Part of a woman's body!

Without further ado, I want to tell you the reason for my good mood.

I have long given up on comparing.

I wish the human mind would never learn to compare.

In my opinion, this is the most useless and, in the long run, the most tedious work in the world, and it will diminish our peace and happiness.

This is the most useless and boring thing in the world, destroying our peace and happiness in the long run.

Wherever comparison enters through any door, enjoyment goes out the other!

Who taught us to compare our organs, faces, and bodies?

The more I look at myself in the mirror and at others, the more I realize that being unique is being beautiful.

I want to call this fact the secret reason for my happiness.

And that is not to compare ourselves with anyone under any circumstances.

Yeah! It's me! A vagina!

Part of a woman's body!

Buy the farewell dress to say goodbye to shame!

I told him that I was ashamed and embarrassed to go to the doctor, to have sex, to do anything that led to being seen.

I often prefer to stay wrapped in several layers of fabric and never be seen by any eyes!

I prefer not to be seen, not to enjoy sex.

My words were not believable to him.

He couldn't believe how I was able to stay in this mental space and condition till now.

At what price was I willing to not feel the pleasures and be deprived and unhappy?

We talked and argued for hours. I knew there was something wrong with me that needed to be fixed. I thought and thought.

Truly;

I had to find out where this shame and embarrassment came from.

What if it's just a temporary sensation?

A solution must be sought.

I thought and thought again.

I finally decided to go to a fancy party, to buy the most beautiful and elegant dress I could see, to name this dress, farewell dress with shame, and shine so well in this dress that I say goodbye forever to the fake shame of my mind.

Now, I am the one standing on the stage. I shine, and when I walk, I look so beautiful that eyes stare at me, and no one knows what is happening inside me.

No one knows about the lock that was on my mind.

Now, I am shining like a queen on this stage,

There is no more tormenting belief or feeling in me.

That's enough... Close your eyes!

Another morning came, and my eyes opened in your eyes.

You look at me like an archaeologist looking at a pure historical artifact. What difference does look at my eyes or my hands make?

At my hair or my lumbar arch? At my genitals or my legs?

Now that we have locked eyes, I want to celebrate it in the best way possible. I want us to look at each other so much that there is no shame between us. You are allowed to look at me as much as you want. Not only will I not feel ashamed, but I want to spend this moment differently with how you look at me.

As our gaze lingers and lingers, my legs go limp; I see the sparkle in your eyes, which now shines differently since you see my vagina. How attractive and desirable it is to you!

It is as if you have known it with all your heart for years.

When you love all of me, as I am, it means peace to me. I understand from your eyes' sparkle that my whole being is beautiful in your eyes.

I know that if it were otherwise, you would not have looked at me so romantically, so I try to slowly put aside my shame and embarrassment in the real sense; at this moment, I want to surrender my heart to your sea of peace and see where the wave of your hands will take me.

I believe that you love everything about me.

My hair, my skin color, my vagina, and everything that evokes me in your mind.

That's enough for tonight. Close your eyes for a while. Don't look into my eyes so much; my legs got weak.

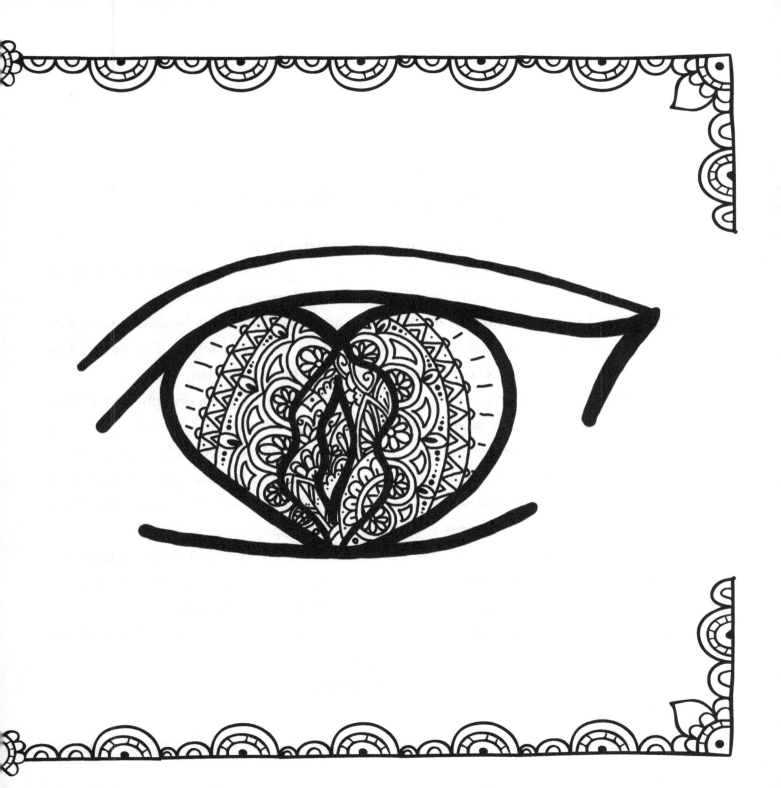

Two by two makes four!

Now, I am in the most satisfactory state.

For this satisfaction smile, I've had several annual checkups, in addition to studying and researching, and I've gained confidence in my health.

I've learned about my internal and external anatomy. I observe hygiene and health tips. I read and researched a lot about choosing a healthy partner. For hours, I've asked experts about sexual relations with men.

Regarding the quality and manner of sexual intercourse, I know enough, and I have no shame or fear of sexual intercourse or sex, which is my natural right.

I've done trial and error on the pros and cons of my related products. I know all the necessary information, from sexual hygiene to menstrual hygiene (period), and even choosing the type of underwear. I've not involved myself in careless and baseless words without scientific support.

Instead, I've tried to provide only the best for myself. I've not followed anyone's advice and experience. Instead, I've exposed myself to new scientific and updated information and professional doctors and specialists.

This satisfaction, smile, health, and well-being come from the peace I have striven for.

Wish you the same.

A cradle hug...

No matter what happens in the outside world, I am always here.
I love myself and take care of myself.
Imagine me sometimes: A safe and constant hug, here, right below, covers your
feminine and sensitive organs with kindness, day and night.
Think of me sometimes, about how I go through hormonal and physical changes during
my periods and how, with the broad flexibility I exert, I still tenderly care for the
innards.
Be like me sometimes. Just hug yourself and take care of yourself. Take care of
everything that fits in your arms, everything you have, your whole self.
I am not human, but I know well the meaning of giving hugs and security. I am not
a butterfly, but I have tiny wings to open to enjoy myself and you and close to take
care of my internal organs.
I am not a cradle, but I provide a warm and moist bed for intercourse so that you can
experience the best pleasures easily and comfortably in my safe space.
While in this bed, I have prepared a safe place for the health of the internal organs
after the vagina. I was created to take care of myself and your femininity.
As long as you want, I will close the path of everything other than your health and
wishes by hugging myself.

Now some peace...

At this hour of the day, I'm in the middle of a bath. Immersed in steam, water, and foam, all the cells of my body are at peace.

Imagine a beautiful old bathroom made of natural rocks and stones.

Healing plants are growing in the corner of the bathroom, and the sound of water is dripping from a gray hand-made stone tub. On the other side, the sunlight reached the corner of the bathroom in the form of several large lines from the wooden window, and the dance of water vapor in the window's light was spectacular. My skin is getting wet by this moisture.

In a brown wooden cage, you can see some natural soaps and body lotions in a milky and creamy color and spring flowers with sweet almond oil or the heavenly aroma of coconut.

I know using them makes me feel better.

I smell the oils.

It is as if they are taking me to a garden of almond and coconut trees.

Or maybe the scent of cherry blossoms and the joyous juice of oranges in soft pink and orange makes me intoxicated and mesmerized by the smell of nature.

I try to use the most natural and healthy oils and creams.

After washing and moisturizing, I put on comfortable cotton underwear that has been sun-dried or ironed. It is clean and free from contamination.

Finally, thank you, yes! You! For providing me with a bed of health and cleanliness.

And me? I will rest in a warm, soft, clean cradle while you do your job.

I am sure that if I am healthy and you are sure about my health, society will be more peaceful.

Everyone is their own color!

Listen! The sound of the waves is heard one after the other.

Here I am, resting on the sand.

I feel the heat of the sun, not directly, but well.

On this beach, we are all relaxing and enjoying a sunny day.

I look at everyone preparing a good day for «herself» yes, only for herself.

On the bed of clean sand, you can see colored mats, beautiful and colorful umbrellas, and delicious and cheerful drinks.

Today, every color that comes to my eyes is beautiful.

Today, every shape, every form, and «every kind of being» is beautiful. None of us are alike.

This diversity and colorfulness have turned this beach into the most beautiful and colorful poster that can be seen.

I close my eyes.

I imagine watching the beach from above.

This sight would not be so spectacular if we were all the same color. It was like an empty beach. It's like a camp where everyone is forced to wear a uniform.

We followed a rule and were all that they wanted. How sad!

Now, I open my eyes again and see that being unique is the best way to live. Being yourself will be very respectable and, at the same time, beautiful and praiseworthy.

On this colorful and sunny beach, everyone is attractive in any shape and form and deserves to relax!

Close your eyes and touch me

One of the best ways to get to know any object is to touch it.

Even if we read hundreds of pages of books about a subject, this information will not be complete until we see and touch that subject clearly.

I know that everything is created carefully and calculated. My body parts that need more care have thicker skin. Some parts have thinner skin due to more sensory nerves. So that I can better enjoy the sense of touch in those parts.

To get to know the hair on my head, my skin, and my vagina, I touch them.

Some parts of my genitals, like other parts of my body, have thicker skin, and some parts have soft and thin skin. Some parts have hair, and some parts have no hair.

It is better for me to know my vagina and genitals first so that I can give my spouse/partner more accurate and better information about myself and my body. Besides reading and talking to my doctor, one of the ways to get to know my vagina is to feel it.

Touching the vagina with the hand is pleasant; by touching my body, I give this message that I love all the parts of my body, and this leads to a more accurate and better knowledge of my body.

Unknowns are always strange and distant, but as soon as I, as the owner of my body, know my whole body, I find a sense of intimacy and friendship with it. What better feeling than conveying the good feeling of care and love to every part of my body?

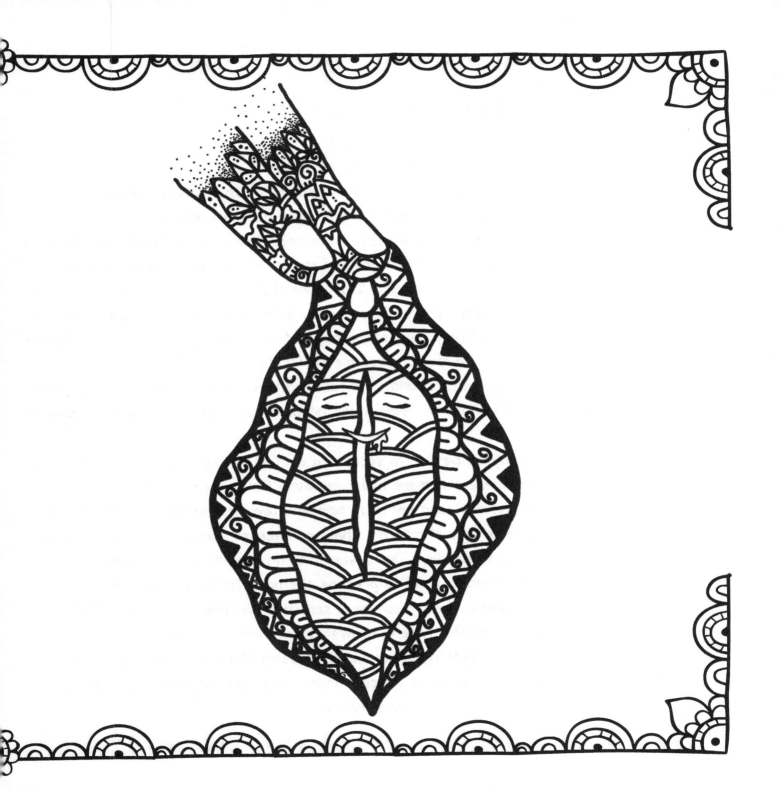

Everything is in order here!

Tik Tak!

Everything is in place here.

Like the gears of a clock that work together for the same purpose.

But it seems that everything is more accurate here!

Like a factory that automatically and without supervision takes several goals and does its job. Any impending problem gives me signs and symptoms to take steps to improve.

I feel comfortable with each of its cells. I am sure that even when I have forgotten her, she has continued her work correctly and accurately, and her whole goal is for me to be healthy and enjoy life. Every day, according to time, events, or things that happen to me, it gives me flexibility.

Taking into account my age, mental and physical conditions, and even my nutrition until my period, pregnancy, and childbirth, everything happens here regularly and in an orderly manner.

For example, today, it may be better to secrete a certain hormone more or less so that my vagina environment is more moist or warm for a specific purpose.

Today may be my ovulation day, and my body temperature and metabolism will increase.

Or the day may come when it is the turn to hold and secure the cells that will become an embryo. During these days, housewarming and periods are prohibited.

Everything goes hand in hand to prepare the best for new conditions.

To coordinate all these events, there must be a sensitive and precise order and planning.

Tik Tok. Listen! The time is «now» at the time of my vagina!

It means that everything in my vagina is being planned for today.

I have just realized that there is a precise order here, even in what I perceive as asymmetry!

I hope my health is good!

When we went to the gynecologist's office for the first time, I knew that since I am 21 years old and sexually active, I should do a pap smear test sometimes. This is exactly where the story of our friendship began.

I was waiting under the lamp's light for my doctor to come and examine me. When she entered the room, I saw that she had a device in her hand and was moving it towards me; at that time, I did not know what it was called.

As «Speculum» approached me, I noticed that it had something like a big beak and was trying to say something with its kind smile. I tried to read its lips and realized that she was trying to tell me to take a deep breath and relax my muscles.

As my doctor was telling me:

My dear, you should do this test once every 1 or 2 years until you reach the age of 30, and every 3 years after the age of 30. I said very quietly, oh, yes, wow... Yes, for sure...

And I was listening to the rest of her explanations when I noticed a new friend coming towards me. With a deep breath, the little «swab» reminded me not to hold myself tight and to be free. When she entered the beak of the speculum oh, the pain was much less this time.

I told my doctor that it was over and she said: Yes. I said: Was that it? How great ...

She said: Yes, my dear, that was it. Instead, you will know that your vagina and mercy are healthy for a year or two. The good feeling of health assurance cannot be replaced by anything. She was right. When the results of my test come and I am relieved that my baby's uterus and vagina are healthy, I have no more worries and can live a healthy life.

Forgotten smells!

Like the forest that smells like a forest. Like wood that smells like wood and apples that smell like apples, the vagina also smells like a vagina.

A member that is with me in cold and heat, sitting and standing, exercising and resting. A healthy vagina is not supposed to smell like perfume and cologne or flowers and chocolate.

We are used to dividing many things, including the scents and smells around us, into two categories: pleasant and unpleasant. We are unaware that this category can only be a matter of taste or related to our good and bad memories. In this black-and-white category of ours, natural scents and perfumes have no place.

We have forgotten being natural and virgin. Our deep breaths have always been in nature, just when there is no empty space for any perfume or essential oil bottle.

Like the smell of hair, body, sea sand, and maybe the smell of delicate and thin feathers of a few days old chicken, which can be special in its own kind.

Specificity means that this scent is completely pure and has not benefited from the intervention of aromatic substances.

It means being yourself...

The vagina is the most feminine organ of every woman, which repeats health and normality every day, and on days of the month, even when it is not during the period, it accompanies us with the natural secretions that are necessary for our sexual health.

This time, I want to smell some of the things that I came across and found out that they are not artificial, with a wider perspective. Like the smell of the leaves in the pot in my house, or even the smell of the peel of fruits, each of which is different from the others, and this pencil even, that is, the pencil in my hand, has its own smell, which is neither good nor bad, it smells like a pencil.

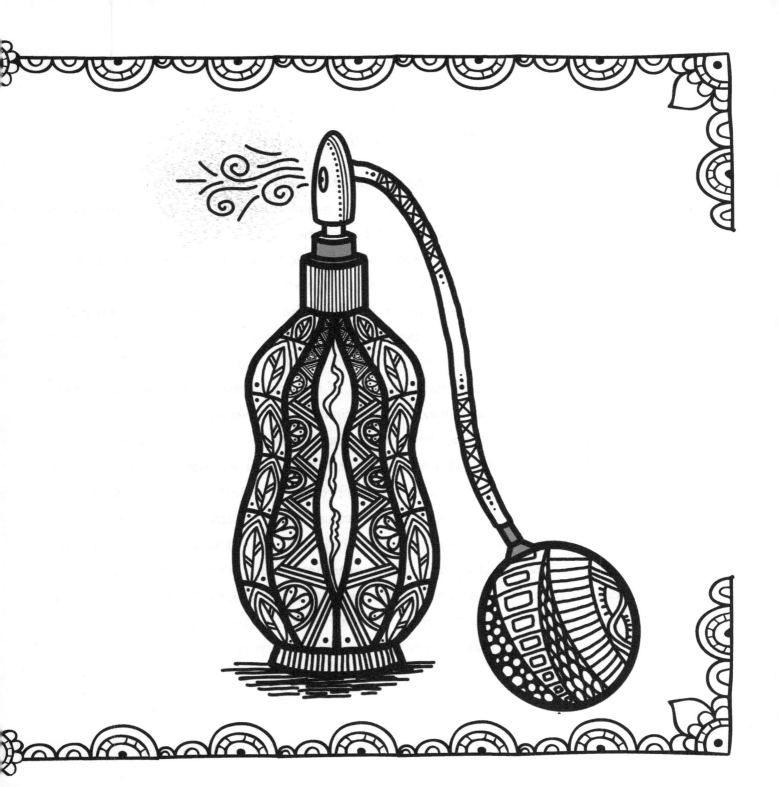

Pull the curtain aside.

From another point of view:

With a deep breath, she opens her eyes like a mermaid among the waves, stretching her body in a sea of white and clean silk sheets.

She gets out of bed, goes to the window, pulls back the curtains, and opens the window. She looks at every beautiful part of this landscape.

From the window curtain to the wooden frame and the curtains that have been pulled aside to the sun that shines on this beautiful view; To the green and palm trees that have grown to the sky thanks to this sun and this sea.

She smiles and thinks to herself as if the sun of this beautiful clitoris land and these curtains and windows are similar to my vagina.

If the sun is not there and does not shine, the pleasure of seeing this view and its beauty is not possible for me. It's as if I have a sea inside me that always keeps my uterus and vagina moist and protects the internal parts, which are like these trees and the island, with its secretions when necessary.

The creator of this landscape has put everything in the right place. She closes her eyes, takes a deep breath, and appreciates her vagina with all its features.

She has placed a beautiful landscape inside herself and is filled with wonder from this order. I just want to be able to enjoy my inner world. With a body that belongs to me and was created for my enjoyment.

We have bunches of flowers in this garden!

Here is a flower garden.

We have all kinds of flowers available here!

Like different flowers that are all beautiful despite their differences.

And like every flower, whose components are different from others, but all of them are called flowers. Each of these flowers is placed in its place and in the way it should be.

Can beauty be taken from a flower?

Or can all flowers be the same?

My sexual organ (vagina) is like any flower, unique and beautiful.

Just like my fingerprint, like my face or body.

In this big world, there is room for all differences.

These differences have made our world colorful, diverse, and beautiful.

So, in this world, I love everything that has been given to me. I know well that if «I» am like «you», I am no longer «me».

And I know that «you» know this truth well.

In this big garden, every flower has its place.

It should remain where it grew and as it is.

Each of these flowers is special, beautiful, valuable, and lovely for themselves.

Each flower has different components such as petals, stamens, stems, leaves, etc.

And how interesting that none of the flowers in any of these components are alike.

Each one has its own unique and beautiful color and shape.

Sound...camera...off...!

I am the most beautiful member of this land. The land of your body!

With any race and color, it is me who is the founder of your entry into pure moments.

I am with you the best pleasures. From love to birth and motherhood... Come with me. Let go of yourself right now and take a deep breath.

Enjoy! it's your right. You are the king of this land. With a comparative view and an eye that is like a camera, only a part of this event is recorded. Don't look at me... It's like watching a movie. If you keep your eyes open for only one part of this story, be sure you will miss the rest of the movie. You stare at a part of the «whole» and miss the whole interesting story that is passing in front of your eyes. Close your eyes this time and feel all of me. So deep that when you open your eyes, you remember the taste of the pleasure you took. All these moments are for you, your share.

This body is dear. Everything is beautiful. It is peace and peace...

Leave everything that takes me in the form of «but» and «if». It has been proven to me many times that others look at me with the same eyes that I look at myself.

This means I can change my view angle to improve the quality of my moments.

In this case, my eyes look at all the beauties together, sometimes I even look with my eyes closed. I love these delightful moments that have been gifted to me unconditionally.

I am in the right place. Allow me to be with the same quality as I should. With all the qualities I have.

I smell a rat; there's something fishy going on!

No matter how I calculate, some things don't add up.

I leave the ruler and drawing paper on the desk and go to the flower house in the yard to calm my mind a bit. We have about a hundred kinds of flowers and plants in the greenhouse. Just as I am thinking about the diversity and abundance of the number of plants, my attention is drawn to the asymmetry of all the leaves and their lack of pairs!

No leaf is the same size or shape as the adjacent or opposite leaf. I smell a rat; there's something fishy going on!!

My mind gets confused and I return to my room.

How many months have passed?

I think and think... I read... research... check...

I'm not getting anywhere with the tools I have! It's like I'm tired of the world of ruler and pen and conveyor.

I'm tired of centimeters and millimeters, and I'm fed up with grid paper and pattern paper.

I hate numbers, figures, calculations, and «why» and «how»

I put all these tools and these thoughts in the drawer of the sanctioning table and close the door slowly.

No, wait! I think a little more. I open the drawer and I want to put the glasses I am wearing in my desk drawer. Invisible glasses are called the same angle of view or type of attitude.

This life is not a place for measurements, numbers, rulers, and geometry.

This life is just a place to enjoy.

I get up…. I go to the greenhouse in the yard to calm my mind again.

How beautiful every leaf in our greenhouse is. Wow, how much I enjoy the disorderly world, each of which is full of reasons and rules.

I go back to my room. How much I love the maze of my body parts—the curves that, until yesterday, I thought were unbalanced or asymmetrical, and I was about to hand them over to the surgeon!

Now I know very well that there is a right and proper answer for every reason in every part of my body.

And I am the one who has the duty to know my body well. Now, you say:

What have you done for yourself, your body, and your reasons?

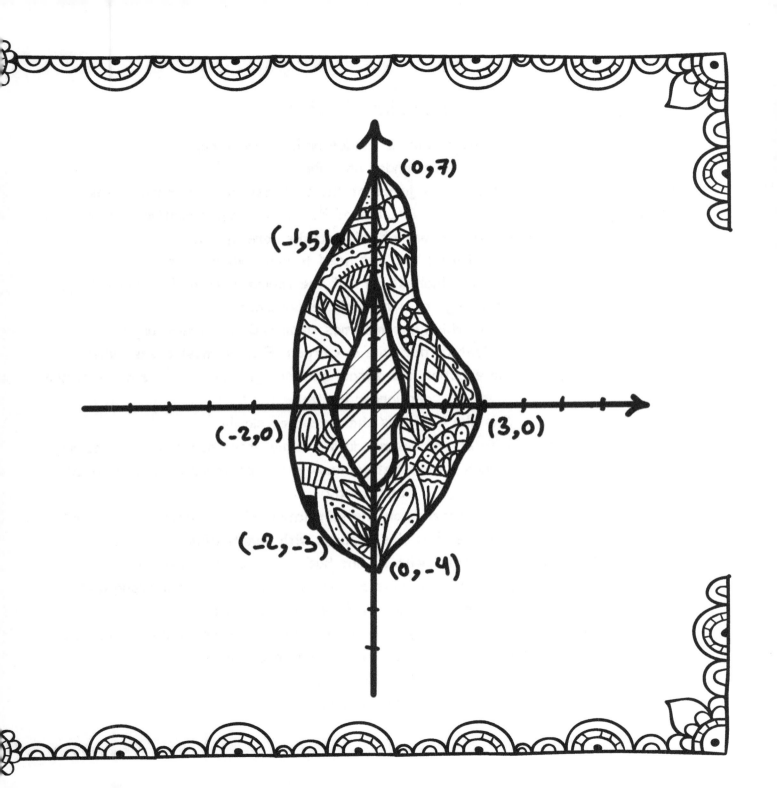

(0,7)

(-1,5)

(-2,0)

(3,0)

(-2,-3)

(0,-4)

C like clitoris that...?!

C like clitoris that is hidden under a small cap;
Lives under an umbrella.
It is so sensitive and vigilant that jumps at the slightest touch or sexual sensation.
And water flows from her mouth... Because of its delicate and sensitive nature, it is hidden under a roof of skin to take care of itself.
C like the clitoris; We just need to know where it is.
The clitoris is located in the highest part of the vaginal area and causes a large percentage of a woman's sexual pleasure.
C like the clitoris, which is sometimes small and sometimes large.
The clitoris is equivalent to the male sex organ. Even in most cases, when stimulated, it may get an erection like a male genital organ and become a bit firmer and larger in size.
C is like a clitoris that prepares slowly.
Because of the sensitivity of the clitoris during sexual intercourse, it is necessary to follow this path in such a way that we know it will be touched or stimulated sufficiently.
Satisfaction in most women depends on the stimulation of the clitoris. This is when most believe that this happens with penetration.
C like a clitoris that I wish no one had anything to do with it.
Still in some countries or even parts of our own Iran, there is a wrong and dangerous tradition of female circumcision.
This has no benefit other than physically harassing the woman, and it becomes a problem for the woman's body and soul.
C like clitoris that...
Now you say...!

What do you call it

The vagina is the outermost sexual organ of my body.

Before I knew it, the vagina, like other parts of my body, had a very high diversity; I always thought it must be something special! A form other than what it is now. Later, by studying and seeing different photos, I realized that there are different types of shapes, sizes, and colors of the vagina, as many people, and different faces as we have. In this big world where there is a reason for everything, one of the uses of the vagina is that it is the entrance to the box of secrets, which I think can be said like this: vagina consists of 4 letters:

«Safe entry of genes»

This organ is the entrance door to a dark, warm, and soft sanctuary where many things happen and humans may live. Therefore, several small and large doors are necessary to protect the internal organs and maintain the health of this environment. Labia majora and labia minora; With the overlapping of the labia and even the small labia not being the same size, irreplaceable security and protection happens. However, make sure you take an umbrella, I know it's sunny now, but better safe than sorry! Some people have a similar feeling of shame to use the name vagina. While the vagina, like the rest of the body, has its own name.

I have heard that in the past and even these days, parents used names for their children's genitals in order to teach their children that it's a private organ, which subconsciously caused them to feel shame and guilt and sometimes even fear touching the genitals. At the same time, the care and privacy of the sexual organ can be taught in other ways.

In order to keep my vagina healthy, apart from the annual checkup, I sometimes feel and look at, and even smell its secretions to ensure the health and hygiene of my sexual organ.

Made in the USA
Las Vegas, NV
05 December 2024